Create THE LIFE YOU
Imagine

WHAT ARE YOU WAITING FOR?

THREE SISTERS

Tracy Flynn Bowe, Kate Flynn, and Meg Flynn

THREE SISTERS
PUBLISHING HOUSE

Three Sisters Publishing House, Ltd.
32104 County Road 1
Saint Cloud, Minnesota 56303
www.threesisterspublishing.com

ISBN 10 0-9785570-1-8
ISBN 13 978-0-9785570-1-0

Printed in the United States of America
First Printing

Design by Donella Westphal and Earl Sorenson
Cover Photo by Jerry Currey
Printing by Sentinel Printing, Saint Cloud, Minnesota
Lead Vocal Performances by Kate Flynn and Jill Moore
Keyboards and Instrumentation by Don Fortner and Pearl Christenson
Recording and Engineering by Rockhouse Studios, St. Joseph, Minnesota

CONTENTS

Acknowledgments

We wish to thank and acknowledge those who have moved us forward on our path and assisted in this creation:

To Tamera Farrand, publisher of Among Women Magazine, for making us a home in your magazine and encouraging our work as teachers and writers;

To Dr. Carol Ritberger, our teacher, mentor, colleague, and friend, for your willingness to follow your path, to encourage us in ours, and to join us in Minnesota frequently along the way—and to Bruce Ritberger for keeping us all on the ground;

To all of our SEND students, for your willingness to show up, do your work, and manifest so powerfully the miracles of personal transformation;

To Stefanie Okeson, Lisa Dempsey, Geno Beniek, Cyndi Silva, Donella Westphal, Mary Kelsey, Lisa Bartholmy, Sara Kubu, Jill Moore, Don Fortner, Earl Sorenson, and Dave Hinman, for all your incredible skill and support in bringing our work into the world;

To our parents, grandparents, aunts, uncles, and cousins, for providing such a rich and diverse family legacy of education, leadership, and service rooted in Benedictine spirituality and values;

To all of the writers and teachers who inhabit the pages of this book, for your work in paving the way and providing light for the journey;

Finally and most importantly, to our partners and children for your love, support, and unending patience with the "sister calls."

In memory of our brother
Michael John Flynn
1960-1998

INTRODUCTION

We live in a culture that is obsessively focused on the external life. At this time in history, an external focus causes most of us to feel out of balance, out of sorts, or completely out of control. The news is filled with stories of terror attacks and natural disasters which hit closer and closer to home. Our technological advances drive us into ceaseless productivity and never-ending demands on our time and attention. We eat in our cars; we are never far from our cell phones, blackberries, or laptops; and we are constantly bombarded by advertising that pushes us to focus more and more intensely on acquiring things in the external material world. Time has become a precious commodity, and for most people it moves faster and faster, leaving seemingly less and less of it available for the things we say are important. We can't pay attention to ourselves, and we find it harder and harder to pay attention to our spouses, children, aging parents, friends, and neighbors, much less the poor, dispossessed, and suffering around the world.

The proposed solutions to all of our problems, challenges, or struggles are also always outside of us: a new gadget, a new wardrobe, a new diet, a new time management plan, a new house, a new co-worker or boss, a new job, a new spouse, a new doctor, therapist, or financial expert. We live in a culture which has conditioned us to look outside ourselves to find all of our answers, our security, our happiness, and our peace—and all the while, we are experiencing epidemic rates of insomnia, attention disorders, anxiety, depression, and suicide. And these epidemics aren't just ravaging the adult world; we are increasingly seeing these diagnoses in our children. More children take medication for psychiatric disorders than ever before. Our teenagers don't want to grow up and take the next steps into adulthood because their parents' lives look weighed down by burden, responsibility, and quiet desperation—completely void of spontaneity, imagination, creativity, and joy.

So how do we live in the material world without losing all connection to ourselves in the process? Philosophers and wisdom teachers from all of the spiritual traditions point us toward the inner life as the only ground from which to live our lives with the compassion, creativity, consciousness, and connection that are the essence of who we are as human beings. When we live from the center of our inner life, we watch the world with "soft eyes" and listen deeply to the inner voice that is trying to get our attention. When we live from the center of our inner life, we know how our body feels and what it needs to be healthy and strong. When we live from the center of our inner life, there is time for reflection, gentleness, and compassion with our self and with others. When we live from the center of our inner life, we make choices with our heart and not just our head. When we live from the center of our inner life, we remember that we each hold divine light and love at the center of our being and are here to move that force into the world.

2

Throughout history, many of those that were interested in following the inner life did so within the protection and nurturance of a monastic community. In a monastic environment, there is time for solitude, reflection, and contemplation built into the fabric of daily life. There is a balance between time in the inner world and time in the outer world. There are also external cues and reminders that call one out of the outer world and into the inner world. Sacred symbols, hourly bells, candles, incense, and silent spaces all remind inhabitants of the monastery of the sacred presence of the inner life. Monasteries can teach us much about entering the inner life.

Our mother encouraged us to see that in this era many of us are called to live like mystics without monasteries. We are called to be "in the world without being of the world" as Jesus taught. We are called to manage the demands of daily life—the job, house, finances, and other responsibilities—without forgetting who we are in the process. We are called to develop a relationship with our inner life that provides the balance and stability we need for our outer life. But most of us don't have a clue what an inner life looks like. We have been pulled so completely into the external world that we no longer know what it feels like to be present in the moment, in our bodies, in awareness and connection with our inner life. We have lost our familiarity with our inner landscape and have forgotten to ask the questions and to seek the answers that really matter.

Our Western scientific materialism of the past several centuries has directed our attention only to the body—the mechanical parts of us that can be seen, measured, x-rayed, and exposed through our instruments of science and medicine—and ignored the more subtle, invisible energies that have been recognized by Eastern medicine and culture throughout the ages. But even in the West, our spiritual teachers have encouraged us to see our essence with softer eyes. Christian Theologian Teilhard de Chardin reminded us that "we are not physical beings having a spiritual experience but spiritual beings having a physical experience." Although we have mastered the visible world in many respects, we have forgotten our nature as spiritual beings and our connection to an invisible world that is bigger than us. James Hillman, one of the great psychologists of our times, suggested that the task of any great society is to keep the invisibles visible. If we are to live in this world without becoming cut off from ourselves, from each other, and from our divine source, we must shift our attention to the invisible world that resides within and around each of us and begin to bring our visible world forward from within rather than from without.

We invite you to interrupt the hypnosis of the outer world and begin cultivating a relationship with your inner world, with your true self, with your soul. Entering into your inner life begins with a simple acknowledgement of the deeper aspects of yourself and a commitment to spend some time each day in the presence of that deeper self. It means acknowledging with gratitude the things in your life that are working and listening from the inside out about the things that need to change. It means surrendering the idea that all the answers are outside of you. It means remembering that within you is a source of wisdom and knowing that can help you navigate your life in integrity with your deepest imaginings. You can create the life you imagine. What are you waiting for?

4

Create

1

PASSION • PROCESS • AUTHENTICITY • SPONTANEITY

I must either commit suicide, or I must give birth every day.

—Otto Rank

Otto Rank was one of the renowned psychologists of the early 20th century. He was a contemporary of Freud and was considered one of Freud's most brilliant disciples. After almost 20 years in Freud's inner circle, Rank broke away to pursue a more spiritually-centered approach to psychotherapy, becoming one of the great pioneers in the fields of humanistic and transpersonal psychology. Rank believed that the essence of a human being is creativity and that understanding ourselves as creative agents in our lives is central to our emotional and spiritual wellbeing. His startling quote suggests that through our creativity we give birth to more and more of ourselves every day, while ignoring our creative power is tantamount to suicide.

Many of us are suffering from our culture's failure to attend to our creative nature. Kate observes that in tough economic times schools are cutting music, art, and drama. Meg finds traditional psychology often ignoring the power of creativity, dreams, art, and imagery as a means of understanding and relieving emotional suffering. Our brother Chris, a physician, complains that medical treatment is being prescribed by insurance companies rather than practiced as a creative art by healers with enough time to understand the meaning and origins of illness. And it seems that everyone is feeling pressured by the demands of working, parenting, and surviving in an increasingly fast-paced and over-scheduled world. These cultural patterns are leading to the despair and suicide of our inner lives and are manifesting with more and more frequency in our outer lives as depression, anxiety, addiction, and physical illness.

Understanding our creative power and potential is the antidote for what ails us. Great teachers from the fields of psychology, spirituality, and philosophy have all recognized the creative essence of the human being. Theologian Matthew Fox maintains that creativity is humanity's greatest gift and that it is spirituality's task to encourage our *holy imagination*. Today's science is also confirming that creativity is a force that courses through the universe. According to scientist Brian Swimme, we live in an intelligent, self-organizing—and yes, creative—universe where if you "let hydrogen gas alone for thirteen billion years, it will result in rose bushes, giraffes, and human beings." Today the scientists are teaching what the ancient mystics and philosophers have always taught—that our thoughts create our reality. If we are to learn to harness our creative power, we must first understand the nature of the divine universe in which we exist.

Einstein and the modern proponents of quantum physics teach us that we live in a quantum universe where the essential nature of the material world is energy. We are told that each of us is 99.99999%

invisible particles in motion rather than solid material form. Yet those invisible particles create and hold together forms through which we can experience ourselves and the material world via our five physical senses. In a quantum universe, moment-to-moment experiences in the physical world emerge out of an infinite set of possibilities and are drawn into physical reality by the simple act of our attention. In a quantum universe, we are asked to accept uncertainty as an operating principal, where events in the material world are not always logical, linear, or predictable but come into existence in quantum leaping patterns that don't exist at all until we focus our consciousness in the act of observation. In a quantum universe, events in the external world are influenced by consciousness itself, in a sea of energy being moved by thought and intention.

The magic of our times is finding the mystics of old and the scientists of today teaching us the same truths about the essence of the cosmic mystery. Poets, philosophers, and mystics have told us for eons that we create our own reality, that our thoughts and beliefs create and draw toward us experiences in the physical world that reflect our consciousness. For example, if we believe that "it's a cold hard world out there," we will draw toward us experiences that evidence and perpetuate that belief. If we believe that we are victims of a random universe with no control over our lives, we will have repetitive experiences of being victimized. And now our scientists are explaining that, in a quantum world, consciousness itself draws forward from the infinite set of possibilities the events that occur in our moment-to-moment experiences. Scientists are telling us that our experiences are directed by our perceptions and that our perceptions are nothing more than internal constructions of reality based on conditioned thoughts and beliefs. Thus, we create our own reality.

Whether we pay attention to the scientists or to the mystics, we learn that we are all constantly co-creating in this quantum dance. We create experiences at our individual level, and we create experiences collectively through the force of group consciousness. This truth suggests that, perhaps now more than ever before in history, because of the powerful global communication networks connecting us all in a global consciousness, our collective imaginings have the power to influence the experiences of the world. If we watch the daily news programs we will be inundated with round-the-clock reports of global terrorism, national division, and world violence. If we accept the assumptions of a quantum reality, we must begin to ask whether our collective imagination is calling forth these realities and what would happen if our mass communications broadcasted themes of global community, world peace, and love with the same 24/7 intensity.

In western culture with our preference for the rational and logical, we have exiled our mystics—and with them a sacred approach to life—in favor of a hard-science, reality-based, control approach that assumes the existence of a linear, logical, and predictable world. We see life as a series of incidents and occurrences to be managed and survived, rather than an elegant dance of experiences and interactions designed by a divine consciousness for our growth and evolution. In the great swing in the evolutionary scheme, however, our revered scientists have led us back to the mystery of our existence, and new discoveries in biology, neurochemistry, immunology, and physics are bringing us all back to the mystery of the co-creative nature of the universe.

Although the complicated concepts and theories of quantum physics are more than most of us will care to explore at a deep level, we can begin our own experiments with the basic notion that our thoughts, beliefs, and expectations influence and direct the events in our lives. If this is true, then we can look at the outside events of our lives to get a picture of our inner thoughts and beliefs. And if we are not satisfied with our life experiences, we may want to experiment with the idea that changing our thoughts and emotional attachments can transform our reality in a quantum leap. If we see ourselves as co-creators of our reality, we must pay closer attention to our inner dialogue and begin to notice the space between our thoughts and the events that follow. If our inner dialogue is consumed with fear, judgment, scarcity, and negativity, we are not likely to attract experiences of well-being, acceptance, abundance, and joy. The bottom line is that in a quantum world our thoughts matter; in fact, our thoughts create and influence matter, moment-to-moment-to-moment in our lives.

When we think about our role in this creative process in which we are all participating, we like to use the term co-creator because none of us are living alone in the universe. Our universe is influenced by the consciousness of every sentient being at some level. We do not exist in a vacuum of our own thoughts and beliefs; we each exist in the collective soup of all the thoughts and beliefs being created by all conscious beings. Therefore, as we begin to take our place in the co-created universal drama we must pay attention to the collective consciousness as well as to our individual consciousness.

It is also true that we are not the ultimate Creator. But our scientific exploration of the nature of the universe tells us that we are a microcosm of the macrocosm, sharing in the creative principle of the cosmos. Likewise, our religious traditions tell us that we were created in the image and likeness of the Creator. Thus, we are all creators, reflections of the Divine Creator, but are limited in our humanness by our own capacity to direct and align our thoughts, emotions, and beliefs in what appears to be a complex and chaotic universe in constant motion. When we begin to cultivate a relationship with our inner life, we will notice that the speed with which we experience our lives seems to slow down. We will find that the chaos we experience by reacting to life externally quiets and we feel more peaceful. When we begin to live in alignment with our deepest self—our soul—we lose the sense of crisis and urgency in our lives and replace it with a sense of participation in the unfolding mystery of our creative dance with God.

As we begin to tune into our power as co-creators, we will also undoubtedly notice that the quality of the intentions we hold for ourselves have more power if they are aligned with the qualities of the Divine. Thoughts that create feelings of laughter, love, gratitude, wonder, hope, compassion, connection, abundance, awe, and joy are grounded in and infused with the energy of the Divine. When we choose thoughts that resonate with these divine qualities, we bring ourselves into alignment with the creative power of the universe and support the emergence of experiences that mirror these qualities in our lives.

If we accept the idea that our thoughts create our reality and that we are thinking all of the time, then—whether we are conscious of it or not—we are creating all of the time. It is obvious, therefore, that to harness our co-creative power in our lives we must begin paying attention to our thoughts. According to the dictionary definition, to "attend" to something means: "to look after," "to be present," "to accompany," "to pay heed," "to take charge," and "to escort." The Latin root of "attend" means "to stretch." As we begin to understand our nature as co-creators, we need to first follow along inside our heads and *be present* to our thoughts. If our thoughts are always creating, as the definition suggests, we had best *accompany* those thoughts and *pay heed* to their potential. If they are not the thoughts we wish to create our next experience, we need to *take charge*, *escort* them to the cosmic recycling bin, and *stretch* ourselves to create some new thoughts.

Conscious co-creation requires that we first develop a basic disposition of self-reflection and self-awareness. If we have never consciously paid attention to our inner life, we will quickly discover that we have very little capacity to direct or influence our thoughts, emotional responses, and beliefs, much less our outer experiences. We will find that our thoughts are on auto-pilot, ruled by unconscious emotions, motivations, and beliefs that are often in chaotic reaction to the external events and circumstances of our lives.

Our first job as co-creators, therefore, is to discover the divine essence of who we are and begin to live consciously from that essence. We need to examine our conditioned thoughts, emotions, attitudes, and beliefs and decide whether they reflect our deepest wishes for ourselves and our greatest potential as human beings. We need to heal our emotional traumas and forgive those that have disappointed, injured, or abused us before we will be able to consciously co-create in our lives. We need to accept responsibility for our choices and behaviors and develop the inner muscle to live in alignment with our deeper selves. We must refuse to live and think reactively because in the process we give away our precious co-creative power to others. In short, we must get conscious before we can expect to direct our consciousness with any measure of success.

If the nature of the universe is creativity and we are all creative beings, we need to ask ourselves if we are creating the conditions we need each day to support our inner life and to construct an outer life that reflects our deepest longings. We must look deeply at our lives and begin to understand that we are the artist creating the landscape we are living. Our thoughts, emotions, beliefs, and repetitive patterns of behavior are working to create the experiences we are living. If we feel like we are prisoners in our lives, we must remember that we are the ones holding the keys. Everything that manifests in our outer life begins with a thought in our inner life. The more time we spend with a thought, the more emotion we attach to it, the more we believe in its power over us and our behavior, the more the thought becomes true in our outer life.

Our creativity lies in the choices we make moment-to-moment as we artistically shape our lives. We can choose to live lives of spirit-deadening routine, boredom, duty, and despair, or we can choose to live lives full of passion and joy. The choice is ours. Perhaps the most precious gift we can offer to ourselves, our families, and the world is to honor our creative capacity and begin—even in small steps—to create the lives we imagine for ourselves and our children.

But how do we interrupt the powerful cultural patterns that encourage us to stay afraid, play it safe, and follow the crowd? How do we begin to creatively give birth to our inner and outer life each day? By asking deeper questions and listening for the answers. By slowing down our schedules to make time for daily silence, prayer, or meditation. By taking a daily walk outdoors, breathing deeply, and focusing on the beauty of the natural world. By planting gardens, cooking meals, making quilts, or painting a room in a color that makes us smile. By laughing, storytelling, playing, or coloring with our children. By shortening our daily lists of should's and have-to's and doing the things that give us joy and bring joy to others. By taking note each day of the things that we are grateful for and imagining more of these things coming toward us each day. By choosing thoughts that connect us with the Divine—thoughts of faith, laughter, love, gratitude, hope, compassion, joy, peace, abundance, wonder, and awe—and noticing how the experiences of our lives change. The world is waiting for you to play your part in the co-creative dance. What are you waiting for?

DREAMS • DESIRES • POSSIBILITIES • POTENTIALS

The privilege of a lifetime is being who you are.

—Joseph Campbell

As we venture into the inner life, we are reminded of the ancient Greek maxim, "Know Thyself." This maxim was said to be inscribed on the Oracle of Delphi temple in ancient Greece in 1400 B.C., and it is also attributed to a number of Greek philosophers, including Socrates himself. This maxim is a wonderful place to begin the journey into one's inner life. As you begin thinking about your life, the first question you must ask yourself is "Who am I?" Not who do people need me to be, tell me to be, or want me to be, but "Who am I?" The answer to this question is central to creating a life that celebrates all of your potential, allowing you to maximize your physical, emotional, and spiritual well-being and to make life choices that reflect your highest possibilities.

In the work we do with our clients and students, we begin answering this question by teaching about the neurology of one's personality. Joseph Campbell said that "the privilege of a lifetime is being who you are," and personality is really fundamental to understanding how we navigate and negotiate our way along our life journey. Personality psychologists and researchers have demonstrated that we all have aspects of our personality that are hardwired from birth. It only makes sense that understanding these core aspects of one's personality is an important aspect of knowing yourself and creating a life that celebrates the most creative parts of your personality.

As you begin thinking about your unique personality, the first question you might ask yourself is whether you are an introvert or an extrovert? When you have a problem to solve, do you begin on the inside by thinking and contemplating or on the outside by talking it through with others? Personality researchers have demonstrated that we are born hardwired with a clear preference for one or the other. In fact, researchers have shown that they can fairly accurately predict whether a child will tend toward being introverted or extroverted by the time the infant is eight weeks old. What these infants show us is that extroverted personalities have an external reference point and direct their attention toward the outer world of people and experiences. Extroverts process out loud and need to talk through their thoughts and ideas to get clarity. In contrast, introverted personalities operate from a more internal reference point and direct their attention toward their inner world of thoughts and ideas. They go inside first to process experiences and need time to think and contemplate before they are ready to talk and communicate their thoughts and feelings. Although we all need to balance time in solitude and time in relationship in order to thrive and grow, if you are an introvert, you need to make space in your life to be alone and to go inside to support your inner growth and development; if you are an extrovert, you need to surround yourself with safe people who can serve as a sounding board when you need to process and make sense of your life.

Researchers have also demonstrated that we have other aspects of our personality that are hardwired. Dr. Carol Ritberger, author of *What Color is Your Personality?*, has developed a personality assessment grounded in the work of Carl Jung that helps people understand themselves better based on these inherent personality traits. Her assessment distinguishes individuals by four personality types or colors—Red, Orange, Yellow, or Green—each of which behaves and interacts in very distinct and identifiable patterns. Personality drives the way we gather information and make decisions. It influences our emotional and behavioral patterns, our relationships, and our approach toward our spiritual journey. In our family, we learned that we had all four colors represented and that we each had strengths and weaknesses based on our personalities. Understanding these differences allows us to understand ourselves and each other more clearly and deepens our relationships with each other. We've included a brief overview of the colors as they show themselves in our family, which may provide you with some clues about your own personality.

The Green Personality: Meg is an extroverted Green—an energetic cheerleader in the personality world. Intuitive, imaginative, creative, and fun, Greens prefer to live life spontaneously, seeking out experiences that ignite their excitement about life. Emotionally sensitive, Greens encourage others to reach for the stars believing that anything is possible. Greens are the "let's experience it all" people who understand their world through their emotions and navigate life using their intuition. They tend to be at ease in the spiritual world and are open to many paths and experiences. Greens trust their connection to all people and things and desire to be a healing force in the world.

The Orange Personality: Kate is an extroverted Orange who focuses most of her life energy on other people. The caretakers and worriers of the personality world, Oranges tend to put the needs of others before their own. Oranges organize social events, volunteer for service projects and committees, and remind us all of the importance of family. Their motto is "if you're happy, then I'm happy." Oranges need the world to make sense and feel right. They are the "let's all get along" people and center their lives on building and sustaining relationships and community. Oranges connect with people easily, tend to be traditional in their faith path, and want to be of service in the world.

The Yellow Personality: Tracy is an introverted Yellow who lives in the world of thoughts and ideas. Insatiably curious, Yellows are life-long learners who love to assist people in solving problems. Optimistic, independent, and self-sufficient, Yellows are often found challenging the status quo and envisioning new possibilities. They are the "let's do it differently" people—creative, intuitive thinkers who spend most of their time mentally constructing and reconstructing reality. Teachers and philosophers at heart, Yellows use their intellect to gain deep understanding about their spiritual life and then share that understanding with others.

The Red Personality: Our brother Chris, an emergency room physician, is an extroverted Red. Practical and detail-oriented, Reds show up, develop a plan, take charge, and finish the project. Reliable, predictable, and organized, Reds know how to operate and negotiate masterfully in the external world. They are the "just-get-it-done" people who measure success on the bottom line. For Reds, life must make sense and be logical—they are the personality type most at ease in the physical world. Reds tend to approach their spiritual life through participation in a traditional faith community, which they support by using their time and resources in tangible ways.

Understanding your personality is the first step to knowing yourself and to making life choices that resonate with the beauty and integrity of who you are. As sisters we have had the gift of developing really deep and intimate adult relationships with each other based on honoring our differences and supporting each other in our uniqueness. Because we are each a different personality color, we understand that we all move toward the same end following different paths and using different processes. If we compared ourselves or made up rules for our relationships that ignored our different talents, gifts, and capacities, we would not be able to create the sacred space for each other that allows us all to grow and develop in the light of our true nature.

The next step to knowing who you are is to begin to take center stage in your own life. Shakespeare reminded us that "all the world's a stage." If we work with that metaphor, awakening to your inner life requires that you begin to see yourself as the central character in your own life drama. Unfortunately, many people view themselves as an extra in someone else's show—their spouse, children, parents, or boss have the leading roles, and they stay on the edge of the stage reacting to each unfolding scene. Worse yet, some people think that they wandered onto the wrong set altogether and spend years feeling completely disconnected from the lives they show up in every day. But as you awaken to the idea that your life is not an accident, that you did not show up in this play by mistake or as a supporting actor, you have to begin to take your place in the center of the stage, creating your life from your deepest imaginings.

When you see your life as a drama you must also see it as a continuous and connected story. Can you accept the idea that there were no mistakes, no missed roads, and no lost opportunities? When you start from this idea, everything that has happened to you or around you takes on new significance and you develop more appreciation for all of the scenes in your life. There may be some scenes from childhood or from an earlier chapter in your life that you have held with anger or regret. But like the flashback scenes in a carefully scripted drama, you can begin to soften your view of those scenes and look for the learning and the lessons that have been unfolding since the opening scene of your life.

You will notice that as you take your place as the lead actor of your own story, you can begin to make conscious choices about the role you are going to play and about the approach you will take in each scene of your life. If you are the lead actor, your thoughts, feelings, dreams, and desires matter, and you begin to shape the direction of your play in ways that support your physical, emotional, mental, and spiritual growth and development. In truth, you will discover that you are not only the central character in the drama, you are also the script writer behind the scenes. You will begin to notice that how you show up in your life influences and directs how others show up in your life and how the events of the next scene unfold. You get to decide if your life story is going to unfold as a tragedy, a comedy, or a heroic journey where you overcome all the obstacles and struggles and create the life of your dreams.

But you must start by remembering who you are. Not the resume you recite to people when you introduce yourself at workshops and cocktail parties, but who you are at the level of your soul. You must go deep inside yourself with the full breadth of your imagination and ask, "Who am I?" If that question is too big, then try these. "Who am I trying to become? Who am I inspired to be? What about life truly feeds my soul and makes my heart sing? What would I do with my life if I had all of the resources I needed, all of the freedom to choose, and all of the support I ache for from the significant people in my life?"

These are questions that require the *holy imagination* of which Matthew Fox speaks. These are questions that have called to the poets and sages of all times. These are questions that the external world most often tells us to put away in favor of more practical concerns. Yet these are the questions we must ask if we are to relieve our feelings of fear, suffering, alienation, and separation. These are the questions we must ask if we wish to create lives of meaning and purpose, connecting ourselves and re-membering ourselves—mind, body, and spirit.

We are here in human form as unique expressions of the Divine.

Each of us holds a seed of the divine mystery as our essence. Our task as human beings is to reveal the divinity within us and to awaken to the divinity in all that is. We cannot begin to express our divinity if we cannot begin to imagine ourselves in a participative relationship with the Divine. Truly, the mystery of the Divine is revealed in and through us, and remembrance of this sacred truth comes at the beginning of any spiritual journey. If we accept that we each hold a seed of the Divine within us, then the hopes and dreams that bubble up from our deepest imagination are not fantasies and illusions but sprouts from the seed of our divine potential. If we accept that we each hold a seed of the Divine within us, then our lives matter, our choices matter, and our dreams matter, and we will take the steps that are required to bring those dreams forward. Each of our stories is the greatest story ever told, and we need to take center stage in our own life drama with consciousness and intention.

The universal truth of the world's wisdom traditions is that we are all participants in the cosmic co-creative dance between Spirit and matter—Spirit moving eternally into the infinite possibilities of matter, and matter moving eternally toward the infinite potentialities of Spirit. To move into conscious alignment with this cosmic dance, we must first understand this sacred marriage between Spirit and form. If we lose ourselves in the material world of survival, grasping, suffering, and attachment, we forget our relationship to Spirit and become cut off from the source of all true power and potential. If we forget our relationship to form, we become entranced by the ephemeral images and imaginings of Spirit and become incapable of bringing Spirit into manifestation through the infinite possibilities present in the material world of form. The challenge of our human experience is to stay fluid in the midst of this cosmic dance, allowing Spirit to move through us into the world as we move in our humanness toward Spirit.

In this cosmic dance between Spirit and matter, we hold a sacred position. We are charged with the responsibility of bringing Spirit into manifestation in the world. We must remember that it is in Spirit that we "live and move and have our being," but it is in form that the mystery of Spirit is revealed moment-to-moment. It is in Spirit where we find our connection to the Divine, but it is in form that we manifest the truth of that connection in our relationship to all beings and experiences in the material world. It is in Spirit that we experience the essence of God as divine love, but it is in form where we move that energy of divine love into action.

The spiritual journey is our movement toward God, and we each have our own path to follow. We each must find our own way to our true Self, to Soul, to God, to the Divine, to the Source. We each come into existence with our own script to write and with many dramas to enact, all inevitably leading us back to the Source of All That Is. While our religious and philosophical traditions can provide a structure for our search, ultimately the spiritual journey is a deeply-personal inner experience that cannot be prescribed or predicted. We can look outside of ourselves and up ahead for hope and inspiration, but we can't find our path by imitating or following someone else's way. The spiritual journey is an inside job, and those who find their way demonstrate a willingness to surrender certainty, to struggle with bigger questions, to engage their *holy imagination*, and to enter into the divine mystery following its call.

The teachers, sages, and mystics of the wisdom tradition have pointed us toward some universal markers on the journey to Spirit. While they cannot lay out the myriad meanderings of the path that are unique to each of us, they can provide a map of the way stations along the journey to assure us that we have not wholly lost our way. A good map can keep us moving in the right direction without dictating stops, side roads, and diversions along the way. In the following sections of this book, we will walk through the markers of the spiritual journey that have been most useful to us and to our clients and students. Remember, we all will travel this path again and again—experiencing, learning, gaining new insights, and rising to higher and more expansive levels of consciousness as we go. As our mother taught us, it is not the destination that is important; it is the journey, and *every step of the journey is the journey*. Imagine a life filled with meaning, connection, peace, and joy. What are you waiting for?

SUPPORT • CONNECTION • RESOURCES • GUIDANCE

Our souls are artistically active in shaping forms of belonging in which we can truly rest and from which our deepest possibilities can be challenged and awakened.

—John O'Donohue

Our mother often quoted W.B. Yeats, the Irish poet and philosopher, reminding us again and again that "life is a mystery to be lived, not a problem to be solved." To truly awaken to the inner life, we must begin to live life from this core philosophy. To live from this philosophy, we must be willing to suspend our attention to the outside world, trust that there are invisible forces holding and directing our lives, and move forward from the inspiration of our inner world. To live from this philosophy, we must approach our life with the attitude of an artist who is here to shape and create our life, not just survive our life.

Western culture favors a rational, linear, and logical "problem approach" to life, where choices about path and passion are strategic responses to external circumstances. The problem approach tells us "it's a cold, hard world out there," and we'd better be prepared for the worst. The problem approach keeps us in reactive patterns, always a bit wary about what tomorrow will bring, clinging almost desperately at times for security in our jobs, our homes, our retirement plans, and our family structures.

But in today's world, it is becoming more and more obvious that there is no real security in external circumstances. Homes can be washed away in natural disasters; jobs and pension funds once thought to be secure for our lifetime disappear overnight with the twists and turns of our economy; divorce, illness, and death change our families without warning; and global and political changes around the world impact us all wherever we live. Many of us have been literally brought to our knees by our struggle with the outside world. But in those moments on our knees, we are confronted with the possibility of surrendering our need for predictability and control and entering into a deeper relationship with the mystery of life and with the imaginings of our inner self.

When we surrender the idea that we can plan, predict, and strategize our way through life, we begin to live the "mystery approach" with the eye of an artist. We once had the opportunity to watch a sculptor working on a block of marble the size of a large room. When we asked about his process for shaping the life-size scenes that he was famous for, he humbly said that the sculpture was already imbedded in the block of marble and that his job was just to patiently chip away at the edges long enough to reveal its true form. His job, he said, was to have an imagination big enough to see the sculpture that was being revealed. This is an example of living from the philosophy of mystery. He knew that the beauty and magic of the sculpture was already present deep inside the raw block of marble and that the outside work was simply a process of allowing the mystery of that inner form to reveal itself.

As our mother and this sculptor wisely taught, when you live your life from the philosophy of mystery, you begin to see life with the eye of an artist, as a creative process where something unseen is revealing itself in each interaction with the outside world. You begin to watch the outside world with soft eyes, seeing the invisible world moving in shadow behind the events that are emerging in the physical world. You recognize that there are no real flukes, accidents or coincidences in your life because everything that occurs is being directed in alignment with your thoughts, emotions, and beliefs. When you open yourself joyfully to the abundant possibilities of your life with trust in the loving support of the invisible world, good things move toward you. When you close yourself off with fear and scarcity thinking, believing that you are all alone and that nothing good is coming your way, you shut off from possibilities and your scarcity thoughts quickly become your reality.

When you live from the philosophy of mystery, you begin to suspend your need for outer security, relying instead on a trust in the process of life to reveal a mystery and magic that is as big as your artistic imagination will allow. You notice that when you show up in your life in a state of open and receptive awareness, miracles occur. Suddenly the external security of a good 401K plan looks like small comfort in comparison to the power and possibilities inherent in the invisible world. You begin to recognize that most people live life with very little imagination and that the deadness many people walk into their day with is a reflection of their unwillingness to trust in the process of life enough to expose their deeper desires and imaginings to the light of day. They bury the wilder, more adventurous, more creative parts of themselves deep within the dark recesses of their bodies and then wonder why their life starts to feel pressed down, lifeless, and constricted. They deny the parts of themselves that are aching for expression and wonder why their body becomes ill and their life loses its spirit. You notice that the more you trust in the process of life, the more life you feel in your body, emotions, and spirit.

When you live from the philosophy of mystery, you power your life from the intention, inspiration, and passion of the inner self with the support of the invisible world, rather than on the will, grit, and perseverance of the outer self. So many of us have been raised in the mindset that emerged from the World Wars and the Great Depression. Our parents and grandparents may have passed forward to us the notion that life is hard and we must struggle and fight against unpredictable forces, holding on by our fingernails to whatever we can grab that feels secure. Many of our religious traditions reinforced this notion, suggesting that the harder the struggle on earth the greater the reward in heaven. But what if you are here to create heaven on earth every day? Jesus said "the kingdom of heaven is upon you." Scholars of the Aramaic language spoken by Jesus teach that there was no separation of here and there, now and then, or earth and heaven implicit in the native language of Jesus. So passive acceptance of suffering and struggle now in this life in hopes of a reward later in heaven would make no sense to Jesus the teacher. You are meant to create your life in its fullness from the profound power of Spirit that is available to you now and at all times. When you rely on your human power alone, you reject the gift of your divine nature and refuse the promise of the invisible world to provide all that you need and to provide it in abundance.

When you live from the philosophy of mystery, you have more capacity to go with the flow, knowing that there is an order and rhythm to life moving you forward in your journey, whether or not you can predict your exact destination. When you work in synchronicity with the invisible world, you surrender your need for a five-year plan, a ten-year plan, and twelve back-up plans. Your security is present in the moment—in the knowing that all things are being cared for and provided for in the invisible world. You realize that your future is emerging from the thoughts and emotions of your present and, the more flowing, receptive, and joyful you are, the more magical the future becomes. You realize that the new experiences arriving spontaneously in your life could never have been imagined by you through the ordinary problem approach, so the plans you make from that perspective become less and less relevant. This is not to say that you give up all of your strategies for living and coping with the realities of life in the material world. You continue to pay your bills, manage your schedule, and care for your family and home, but you do so with the trust and security that come from the inside, rather than the fear and insecurity that come from the outside. You plan from your dreams and desires and not from your worries and fears. You just become more and more willing to be present in the moment in your life—patient with the blank canvas of each day and looking for the magic in each moment—instead of guarding against the problems of your past and the unforeseeable events of your future.

When you live from the philosophy of mystery, you are willing to accept that the struggles of life are like blows of the sculptor's hammer, breaking away the shell that encloses your essence and revealing the deeper and richer expressions of your truest self. You begin to see struggle as a sign that you are holding onto thoughts, emotions, and beliefs that limit you and interrupt the flow of divine guidance in your life. You see struggle as a sign that you have outgrown some old story or belief and recognize it is time to make room for bigger stories and new possibilities. You notice that when you make life hard, when you go into fear, when your body becomes paralyzed and your mind becomes confused, there is some part of you that has become rigid and that needs to be chipped away to make room for your growth and expansion. You realize that, when the struggle with life in the outer world knocks you down, you must seek your answers from the inner world, surrendering your human ideas about what your life is supposed to be and allowing the divine possibilities hidden beneath the surface of your life to emerge.

Irish poet and spiritual teacher John O'Donohue encourages us to see all the events of our lives as meaningful and to settle into the clay of our lives. He says that we all are searching for a feeling of belonging but that the secret to all belonging is to belong to ourselves first. He assures us that "our souls are artistically active in shaping forms of belonging in which we can truly rest and from which our deepest possibilities can be challenged and awakened." O'Donohue reminds us we will never find the rest, security, and belonging we seek in the material world. If we are alone in the universe, then fear of the future is our only motivator, and life will wear us down and wear us out. But if we trust in our divine nature and in our ever present connection to Spirit, then we move into a flow with our true nature, where life presents only more and more possibilities for our growth and expansion. We must all find our rest in the invisible world and in the knowing that we are always safe, supported, and held close in the ever present embrace of Spirit.

As we have followed our mother's sage advice and moved into the mystery approach to life, our shared intention to live lives filled with joy and spirit has revealed possibilities that the problem approach would never have allowed or imagined. We invite you to soften your attachment to the problem approach and begin to adopt the mystery approach as you move into deeper connection with your inner life. Settle into the clay of your own life drama, accept that your soul is directing the play, and allow your deepest imagination to script the next act. Trust in the process of life. What are you waiting for?

REFLECT • SURRENDER • RELEASE • CHANGE

I believe that we should make it a habit to think about death and dying occasionally, I hope before we encounter it in our own life.

—Elisabeth Kübler-Ross

As we cultivate an ever-deepening relationship with our inner life, we will inevitably encounter our greatest human fear—the fear of death. Our Western technological culture has been organized around preventing death and controlling the cycles of nature. We are afraid of changes in our relationships, our jobs, our neighborhoods, our businesses, the economy, and global weather patterns. We live in a culture that fights aging, negates the wisdom capacity of our elders, and uses technological advances in medicine to artificially push the natural boundary between life and death farther and farther away. We clutter ourselves with things, activities, roles, and rules about life that help us to maintain a sense of safety, security, and stability in the visible world. But as we enter deeply into our inner life, we must make peace with the twists and turns of living and nurture our capacity to move fluidly and without resistance with the natural rhythms and cycles of life.

As children we grew up living on a lake in a suburb of the Twin

Cities; now all three of us live on the Mississippi River in Central Minnesota. Living on the river, particularly this river, reminds us daily about the natural flow of life. In the spring, the river is high on the banks from melting snow and spring rains. The birds of the river return and new families of ducks and geese learn their way around. The spring water moves fast and furiously over the dam, carrying tree limbs and river debris swiftly over the surface, yet the current underneath moves steadily and inevitably toward the ocean in the Gulf of Mexico. At this time of year, river boaters know to be wary as they travel, for an unexpected encounter with a hidden log or a newly transplanted boulder will mean sure and sudden trouble for their props. But underneath the surface, the deeper current moves effortlessly and fluidly around these obstacles in a gentle steady flow toward its destination.

As spring turns to summer, the channels and throughways become more stable and predictable. The trees become full, lush, and green. It becomes harder to distinguish the new ducks and geese from their parents as they float leisurely up and down the river. The surface of the river seems to slow down along with the river dwellers who shift into summer mode, slow down their work lives, and spend more time relaxing in the flow of the river. Yet underneath the surface, the deeper current continues its steady movement toward the ocean.

In the fall, the river is lower and slower yet. The ducks and geese leave for the winter, and lower water levels expose new obstacles and present ever-shifting challenges for boaters. The fresh green of summer disappears and the changing colors of fall remind us it is time to pull in docks and winterize boats in preparation for icy winter days. While we all mourn the end of summer, the dazzling fall colors reflecting on the slowly moving water and the stunning beauty of the sun shimmering on new snow while the still-open channel carries ice flows down the river remind us of the unexpected beauty of all the seasons. And even as the waters slow and the river begins to ice over, underneath the surface, the deeper current continues its sure and steady movement toward the ocean.

As we think about Dr. Kubler-Ross and her teaching on death and dying, we are reminded of this river. Each of our lives has a flow to it that cannot always be predicted or controlled. There are hazards and obstacles that expose themselves over time that we each are required to navigate. There are times when the surface of our life seems to be moving fast and furiously and times when things slow to a near stop. There are seasons of life that seem exciting and teeming with new life and times when we must resign ourselves to shedding the old and trusting in the unseen promise of fullness in the seasons yet to come. But our life on the Mississippi River reminds us that there are gifts and hidden beauties during every season of life, and try as we might some days living in Minnesota, we know we cannot expect to hold onto the pleasures of summer during the cold and icy month of January. Our lives move like the seasons—through beginnings, middles, and endings—yet all the while under the surface of our life events, the deeper current of life continues its steady movement toward Spirit.

As we turn inward we connect more and more consciously with that slow, steady flow that is the deeper current of life. We remember that the deepest part of our self—our soul—is always moving effortlessly under the surface of our life in perfect union and flow with the divine. We begin to practice the feeling of fluidity and move without resistance through and around the obstacles and changing landscapes of our lives. We don't metaphorically race our boat up the channel at fifty miles per hour in the spring when our prop will inevitably be knocked out by floating debris. We don't pretend that we can create our own little dam to stop the flow of the Mighty Mississippi downstream. We don't park our boat in the middle of the river, insisting that winter will not come. Instead, we maintain a slow and steady awareness about the unending movement of life and find a way to move harmoniously and without unnecessary struggle with that flow.

The hazards and obstacles of life come in many forms: job changes, economic downturns, family changes, illness, and death. In many ways we all experience death every day. We have to release old ideas and old ways of being that no longer serve us. We have to let go of familiar patterns and stages in our lives—our youth, our children, our physical health, our professional accomplishments. We have to accept changes in the people we love and our relationships with them. We have to release our ideas about how we thought our life was supposed to go when we imagined it at an earlier stage of life. We have to let go of people and situations that restrict or abuse us.

Many of us resist change with all our might. We find ourselves locking down, holding onto the past, and refusing to surrender to the inevitable changes that are moving in our lives. We feel something new coming toward us and anticipate the change with a sense of fear or dread that must be avoided at any cost. But if we remember the

Buddhist teaching that everything in life is impermanent and ever-changing, if we can take a lesson from the wisdom of the river, then we can let go of our resistance to change and loosen our grip on what we know, on what is familiar, and on what seems safe. We can let go of emotions that bind us to old stories and losses. We can let go of disappointment, resentment, anger, and grief. We can recognize that our attachments and negative emotions have become like huge anchors we drag along behind us, holding us back, weighing us down, and getting tangled and encumbered in other people's stuff. We can be willing to "let go and let God" and allow ourselves to move gently back into alignment with the flow of life.

One of the hardest things we are asked to do in our humanness is to let go of the people we love. We lost our brother to cancer at the age of 38 and our mother to cancer at the age of 64. Both of them died too young, and we were not ready to let them go. Our mother held a very central position in our immediate and extended family. She lived her life with an open-hearted and soulful truth that made her a powerful force and a remarkable spirit. Her passing left a hole in the visible world. But our mother was our teacher in death as she had been in life. We spent the day of her passing with her in ritual and prayer. As night came, she made her transition into the invisible world, breaking into a radiant smile that penetrated the room, our hearts, and our grief. It was evident to us in that moment that this was a leaving, not an ending. Kate, who sang to her as she left, said she felt the earth contract in her leaving, as the heavens expanded in a joyful hallelujah at her arrival. Meg, who believed she would not be able to bear Mom's leaving, experienced an unexpected and transcendent feeling of celebration and joy for several hours after Mom's passing. Tracy experienced a deep sense of peace and connection, which filled her heart and softened her sorrow.

Through her life and through her death, our mother taught us with tremendous clarity that the movement of life never ends and that the promise of resurrection is a mystery in which we all participate. There are still times that we ache for the sound of her ineffable laugh or the feel of her strong hands holding us in a loving embrace. But when we listen deeply in our prayers and meditations, when we connect with that deep current of Spirit moving below the surface of the visible world, we realize miraculously that we haven't lost her at all, for she is ever present in the invisible world. The teaching of the resurrection is that even in the wake of the darkest changes and transitions of life, unforeseen and powerful experiences emerge when we are able to let go.

If we are really going to live in alignment with the truest parts of who we are, we must risk staying in the flow with the deeper current of our life. We must surrender to the movement of life in the invisible world and be willing to shed the parts of us that we have outgrown— the things, the people, the roles, the expectations, the false selves, and ultimately the body. We must let go of our attachment to the outcomes of things, to guarantees, and to the certainty we are taught to trust in the visible world. But in the simple act of letting go, we create the space for new things to come forward and become more fully present in the moment to the unfolding mystery of our life. Our mother taught us that changes and endings are part of the river of life and that, in the wake of each little experience of death, something new is emerging to be celebrated and discovered. We invite you to contemplate the parts of your life that are moving and changing. Remember to move through them fluidly like the water of the river, cultivating the ability to be present in all the seasons of your life with as much grace and gratitude as possible. Let go of the old and make room for the new. What are you waiting for?

Believe 5

AFFIRMATION • STRENGTH • POWER • POTENTIAL

*Sometimes it takes darkness and the sweet confinement of
your aloneness to learn that anything or anyone that does not
bring you alive is too small for you.*

—David Whyte

When we begin to trust the reality of the invisible world and let
go of the old patterns of thinking and feeling we've used to organize
our life, we experience a moment of pure exhilaration and relief at
the potential freedom offered by this new way of being. Most often,
however, that moment of exhilaration is followed by a moment of
pure panic. We knew who we were in that old way. We knew the
ground upon which we stood, and it felt familiar and solid. There
was a feeling of comfort and safety in following the ordinary rules
about life, even if they made us feel limited and constricted. Lots
of people in our lives understood us in that old way of being. Our
family members, friends, and co-workers supported the conditioned
roles we had learned to play. But they don't understand our new way
we have of thinking and being; and truthfully, we are not even sure
we do. Suddenly, the feeling of liberation we experienced turns to
sheer terror and confusion. We really don't know who we are when
we let go of the visible world and the safety of our conditioning as

our life compass. It feels a bit like showing up for that first day of high school, college, or a new job—we are surrounded by people, but we feel very alone. We aren't really sure what to believe.

In fairness to us, very little in our culture reinforces or encourages our transition into this new way of thinking and being. When Thich Nhat Hahn, a Vietnamese Buddhist monk and spiritual leader, reflected on his own experience of coming to the West in the 1970s, he remarked that in the West we encounter very few reminders of the sacred presence of the Divine during our daily lives. He noted that in the East they are reminded throughout each day of the divine presence by the sacred symbols, temples, bells, and rituals attached to the activities of daily life, such as waking, eating, greeting, and connecting intentionally and reverently with nature. In the West, we have removed the sacred symbols from our public landscapes, and we race through our days without the interior attention that would call us back into relationship with Spirit. As we have relegated the sacred to the backseat in Western life, most of us have lost the daily rituals that support the contemplative or reflective practices that are essential to developing the capacity to live life with conscious intention in connection with the deeper aspects of ourselves.

As we begin our journey on the spiritual path, we must learn to harness our potential as co-creators and to use this potential with intention and awareness. The ability to act consistently as creative agents in our lives is a developmental process. While Spirit can and does break through spontaneously in all of our lives through the power of Grace, the day-to-day ability to align with Spirit in co-creating lives that support our highest potential as human beings requires patience, attention, discipline, and the active development of consciousness. Most of us hit adulthood ill-equipped to manage our lives with that kind of artfulness, and we generally receive little guidance on how to develop the skills that are required to create a life merging Spirit and matter.

So when that moment of terror strikes, we must remember that learning to live consciously is a developmental process and give ourselves permission to do it step by step. We all know that learning to operate our physical bodies is a developmental process. As infants, we learn to roll over, sit up, crawl, walk, and then run. A two-year-old child can do effortlessly what a one-year-old struggles to do. Growing into our spiritual consciousness is just another step in our developmental process. We first have to master our physical bodies, then we learn to use our emotions and thoughts, and finally we begin to develop our spiritual consciousness.

Ken Wilbur, one of the prominent psycho-spiritual theorists of our time, has developed an intricate map of consciousness and its progression through a developmental model. He teaches that our Western culture and educational structure are designed to move most of us very effectively through the stages of development of our physical, emotional, and mental processes. But as we reach adulthood—when we should be evolving into higher levels of spiritual consciousness—development for most of us stops until close to the end of life or until we experience a major interruption in our lives like illness, divorce, or the death of someone close to us. This can be attributed to the fact that our Western preoccupation with the external world has left most of us unfamiliar if not uncomfortable with the invisible side of life. But if we are going to develop in our spiritual lives, we will have to give ourselves permission to step away from the visible and the ordinary and believe in our connection with the invisible and the extraordinary.

When we decide to take our place as creative agents in our lives, we must think developmentally about progressively moving through stages and developing the "spiritual muscles" to master the developmental challenges of each stage. Much of today's new age co-creation material is accurate in theory but dismisses the developmental work that is necessary to support our co-creative potential. In theory, a toddler has the potential to become an Olympic athlete, but clearly the toddler needs to be supported and coached through the stages of developing that level of mastery in the physical world. In our culture, most of us are spiritual toddlers: we would like to act and create in alignment with our Olympic-level spiritual potential, but we have to develop our skills with consistent practice, discipline, and patience.

In our Western frenzy for immediate gratification, we want to be handed the seven secrets of the universe and immediately go to work co-creating and manifesting lives of richness and abundance within 24 hours. But cultivating a spiritual path is not that easy. Deep inner work takes time and attention. Like the toddler with Olympic potential, we must be willing to learn, train, practice, and master our spiritual life. We must be careful, however, that we don't attack the spiritual life with the savage intensity of some Olympic athletes. We should use the toddler as our model instead. Toddlers master their physical bodies with relatively little struggle and with a sense of joy and ease. As the mother of four children, Tracy vividly recalls watching the magic of her infant children discovering and understanding the movement of their tiny hands. They could mesmerize themselves for hours just watching their little fingers moving, astounded by the fact that they seemed to have something to do with it. Slowly, they mastered getting them into their mouths and then into Tracy's mouth, eventually getting everything in the universe into their mouths with those magic hands. Likewise, when they learned to walk, they squealed with delight at their first shaky steps, and didn't rebuke themselves when they landed on their bottoms; they just got back up determined to try again, all the while enjoying the process.

So as you take your first steps into your spiritual training, begin with the joyful delight of a toddler. Marvel at the extraordinary potential of your spiritual nature. Start to take note of your ability to change things in your outer world with the power of your intention, just like the toddler who learns to manipulate her fingers. Cheer yourself on when you allow yourself to connect with the flow of Spirit moving through you, and don't beat yourself up when you get stuck in old patterns and limiting beliefs—just be aware of it. Because every time you bring a limiting pattern into awareness, you get to make the choice about whether you want to stay there. Moment-by-moment, choice-by-choice, thought-by thought, you get to decide what you believe. If you choose to believe that you are more than meets the eye, you will move closer and closer toward the heart of your spiritual essence, and your life will begin to change.

The beginning of the spiritual training process is to anchor your new beliefs with some practices that strengthen and support your growth and development. If you were going to learn to play the piano, you would undoubtedly be required to practice for at least thirty minutes a day. As you begin your spiritual development, find some kind of daily inner practice for thirty minutes a day. Maybe you do it in two sessions—fifteen minutes in the morning and fifteen minutes before bed—but try to connect consciously with your deepest self and with the energy of Spirit in a regular and rhythmic way. The only way you will become familiar with your inner landscape is to spend time there exploring and discovering. Your practice may include prayer or meditation, journaling, spiritual reading, a mindful walk in nature, or a moving meditation like yoga, chi gong, or tai chi. In the early stages of your development, anything that slows the mind, calms your emotions, and creates a feeling of spaciousness is the goal.

Next, set up some outer structures to support your inner work. As we have learned, your thoughts create your reality, and you need to create tangible forms of support for your new thoughts. You might start in your own home by hanging posters, displaying books, posting affirmation statements, lighting candles, or listening to spiritual music or lectures. You might also find a safe friend or family member that shares your spiritual interest and use them as a sounding board when you have questions or experiences you want to process. At these early stages of practice, you want to choose people that can support you in your exploration and discovery stages without a lot of doubt and resistance. You have all you can do to manage your own doubt and resistance, and adding fuel to the fire will not support your progress. You might also attend a workshop or lecture or take a meditation or yoga class, where you're likely to meet people that are following their own spiritual path. Anything you do in the visible world that can help validate the new things you are choosing to believe about yourself and the universe will strengthen your resolve to move forward in your practice.

Living a spiritual life takes practice, resolve, tenacity, and courage. The early stages are the most difficult because the comforts of the old ways of seeing and believing are so seductive. At the early stages of practice, we are tempted to think it would be easier if we could fly away somewhere or retreat from the world while we find our footing in this invisible world. Yet most of us are called to be mystics without monasteries—finding new ways, asking new questions, and believing new truths in the here and now of our daily lives. As you begin to believe that your life matters, your thoughts matter, and your choices matter, you find the time, the space, and the ground you need to support your life in the invisible world, while continuing to walk in the visible world.

As you continue to journey further along the path, you find yourself looking back less and less often and realizing, when you do, that you can't go back. Because having touched the freedom, spaciousness, and potential of your new life, you really don't want to. In the process of journeying into the inner life, somehow the terrifying feeling of being alone transforms. Poet David Whyte tells us that "sometimes it takes darkness and the sweet confinement of your aloneness to learn that anything or anyone that does not bring you alive is too small for you." If you believe that you are not alone and have never really been alone, if you believe that you are supported and connected to the power of the invisible world at all times, then you will believe you can create a life that is big enough to hold the dreams and passions of your soul. What are you waiting for?

COMPASSION • FORGIVENESS • ACCEPTANCE • CONNECTION

If you take a risk and follow your heart, you will always get more, not less.

—Dorothy Flynn

The Land Beyond Forever was the first book we launched at Three Sisters Publishing House. This book and accompanying CD are about our sacred connection to spirit and are dedicated to the legacy of our mother who left the visible world in October 2002. Tracy received the poetry of this story in a dream inspired by her then three-year-old daughter Anne. While putting Anne to bed one night, Tracy told her stories about her grandmother, wanting her to know the joyful and indomitable spirit who had become ill when Anne was only six weeks old. Tracy finished the stories and told Anne to go to sleep and have a dream with Gran. As Anne drifted off to sleep, she instructed her mom to follow her in her dream, for she knew the way to Gran. Tracy agreed. A moment later, Anne opened her eyes and asked if they should take their bodies with them in the dream. Tracy told her that they could leave their bodies in bed to rest. Anne agreed. A minute or so later she opened her eyes again and told Tracy that she was taking her face with her so that Gran would know who she was. Before drifting off to sleep, Anne opened her eyes one last time and very deliberately said, "Don't lose me, Mom. I'll lead you there."

In her dream that night, Tracy woke up hearing the poem of the story in full form. In the dark, she wrote it down, just as she'd heard it in her dream. Tracy believes that Anne did lead her to Gran in their dream that night and that the poem she received was Gran's message for us all: "There is no death, so follow your hearts and enjoy life in all its wonder!" When the story was illustrated, the magical artist showed Anne and Tracy traveling through the heart on stars of light to meet with Grandma and the other ancestors and great spirits of all time. The message of the book is for children and adults alike: it teaches that we are always connected to spirit and to those we love and we must create lives of joy and inspiration during our time on earth.

As a family, we had to walk through the difficult loss of our brother and mother to cancer, yet following their deaths we have experienced their continued presence in our lives. Our Irish spiritual roots support this sense we have of an ongoing relationship with them. The Celts have always recognized death as a natural part of life. They believe that, in death, those we love slide out of the visible world but remain close by—connected to us and supporting us from the invisible world. In talking with people about our book and our experiences with our brother and mother, we have heard hundreds of stories from people who whisper to us about their own loved ones and their own experiences of sensing, feeling, smelling, dreaming with, and receiving guidance from these loved ones after death. At some level, we all have had these experiences of the invisible world, yet we are never quite certain about whether or not to trust them because the experiences cannot be seen or validated in the visible world. As we awaken to the inner life, however, we are seeking to cultivate a relationship with the numinous and eternal parts of ourselves and to trust that there is an invisible world that supports and directs our lives. It is often during times of suffering, grief, or loss that we connect with a deeper part of ourselves and remember or discover the presence of this invisible world.

Through our most difficult life experiences, we have learned to trust and accept the relationship we have with the invisible world. As we have come to know the eternal presence of those we love, we have been compelled to remember the eternal parts of ourselves. And as we have come into this deeper relationship with the invisible world, we have had to let our lives be directed by our hearts rather than our heads. Our heads demand proof, evidence, and guarantees before committing to change and growth. Our hearts simply know the truth. As our illustrator elegantly showed us, it is through our hearts that we find the doorway to the invisible world, to the seat of our soul. Our hearts know how to respond to the pull of the numinous and eternal calling us to create lives that are rich and full. Our hearts know that life is a gift of spirit and that we are meant to bring spirit into the world through the daily choices we make in our lives.

Scientist and spiritual teacher Joan Borysenko wrote a beautiful poem found in her book, *Pocketful of Miracles*, that also draws us into our hearts as the next step in our spiritual journey.

In the secret recesses of the heart
beyond the teachings of this world
calls a still small voice
singing a song unchanged
from the foundation of the world.
Speak to me in the eyes of a child
you who call me from a smile
my cosmic beloved
tell me who I am
and who I will always be
help me to remember.

Our hearts are truly the gateway to the invisible world and to lives of joy and inspiration. Our suffering, our struggles, and our searching for another way to live inevitably lead us to the doorway of our hearts, where we can choose to find a new way. Some stand in front of that doorway and feel too beaten up and broken hearted to go in. Some say that it hurts too much to trust, to believe, and to love in an imperfect world. They close themselves off in protection—choosing not to love, not to accept, not to forgive, and not to let go of their grief and disappointment—for fear their hearts will just be broken again. But there is a Buddhist teaching that says our hearts are meant to be broken ten thousand times. And with each breaking, our hearts soften, until they break open in compassion and love for ourselves and each other. Jesus said "knock and the door will be opened"; perhaps he was speaking about this doorway of our heart. If we choose to enter into the invisible world through the doorway of our heart, we will open ourselves to love. And all of the wisdom and religious traditions teach us that love is the essence of God and the greatest power in heaven and on earth.

If you walk through the door of your heart, you will hear that small gentle voice telling you all is well. When you are suffering, confused, worried, or fearful, in the stillness of your heart, you will be met with love and compassion. When you are blaming and resenting others, judging yourself, or collapsing under the harsh and critical voices you hear inside your head, in the stillness of your heart, you will be shown the power of forgiveness and self-acceptance. When you are sad, lonely, or grieving, in the stillness of your heart, you will be held in a loving embrace. When you ask to remember the truth of who you are, in the stillness of your heart, the truth of your numinous and eternal spirit will be revealed.

But when you follow your heart, you will at times be pulled toward choices that seem illogical or risky in the visible world. You will be called to hazard yourself in your relationships, your family life, and your work life in ways that threaten your old identity and challenge the status quo that keeps you feeling safe. If you listen deeply to your heart about what you truly long for, it will call you into a deeper, more authentic, and more creative way of living. But it may feel risky to tell someone how much they have hurt you or how deeply you love them; it may feel risky to ask for forgiveness from your child, partner, sibling, or parent; it may feel risky to begin a process of therapy or spiritual direction to heal the sad, fearful, or grieving parts of yourself; it may feel risky to acknowledge that you want to go back to school, change careers, or start your own business; it may feel risky to say that there are parts of yourself that feel numb or asleep in the safety of your current life story.

But when you open your heart to yourself and to others, when you listen to those small still voices, miracles will occur. Our mother used to say that "if you take a risk and follow your heart, you will always get more, not less." She taught us that if we sought to live a life without risk, we would likely never discover the richness and fullness of who we really are. She taught us that we are always held up and supported by the divine presence of the invisible world, and in that world the only real risk is not bringing the fullness of our spirit into being.

We live in times that encourage us to play it safe. But the opening to the invisible world comes when we make the decision to step inside the doorway of our heart and connect with a presence that is large enough to hold not only our fear and suffering but also our divine possibilities. As you continue your journey into your inner life, we encourage you to take a risk and listen to your heart. As our mother said, when you follow your heart, you will always get more, not less. What are you waiting for?

STRETCH • REACH • ASPIRE • INSPIRE

Great wisdom traditions tell us it is possible to go beyond suffering to reach expanded states of awareness where our personal transformation can not only bring joy to us but also heal the larger web of life.

—Deepak Chopra

On October 2, 2006, on a crisp and sunny fall day, a man walked into a one-room school house in Pennsylvania Amish country, shot and killed five young school girls and injured five more before killing himself. Even in the idyllic seclusion of this small Amish community, the violence of this world and of this time exploded into our consciousness as we watched it unfold on CNN in disbelief. Through their actions, suicidal teenagers and addicted, despairing adults from around the world are talking to us all about their intolerable levels of suffering and despair. If we think that our political and military leaders can protect us through a "war on terror" or that a barrage of metal detectors or swat teams at schoolroom doors will keep our children safe, we are being asked to think again.

In his book, *Let Your Life Speak*, Educator Parker Palmer said, "If we do not understand that the enemy is within, we will find a thousand ways of making someone 'out there' into the enemy." It is a shortage of love, compassion, and connection to something bigger than our economics, our personal security, and our fear that is creating the terrorism in this world. What will it take for us to understand that we live in a global community where all of our suffering is connected? When will we start to pay deeper attention to creating lives of meaning and passion that will inspire us and our children to want something more than a trip to the mall? When will we aspire to use our incredible imaginal power to create a vision for individual, family, national, and global peace and wellbeing? Until we attend to our individual and collective suffering and stretch ourselves to ask questions that are big enough to help us reconstruct a world where we can live in authentic connection with ourselves and with each other, the violence will continue to escalate.

The enemy is within, and we are fighting a war against our own crisis of meaning in a world that has lost its spiritual compass. The fix begins "in here," in our hearts and souls, not "out there." Unless we each address our internal feelings of disappointment, resentment, confusion, fear, addiction, anger, hatred, and rage, these unresolved emotions will continue to spill over into our lives and into the world like a plague on our time. Creating a world based on our enormous human potential is possible, but only if we begin to do some things differently.

In the wake of the Pennsylvania school shooting, the Amish community, which had lost its most innocent members to unspeakable violence, came together in prayer with the world watching. They prayed for their slain daughters, for their community, for peace in the world, and for the shooter. They refused the requests of news reporters to speak with blame, anger or judgment about the man who had taken what was so precious. Even further, they arranged a private meeting with the wife and family members of the shooter and met together in forgiveness and healing. One of the Amish fathers present at the meeting said it was an extremely emotional meeting, and "there was a higher power in the room." Through their thoughts and actions based in love and compassion, they reached toward God for understanding, and, in the process, transformed the violence of this tragedy by refusing to continue moving hatred and terror into the world. Less than six weeks after the shootings, the world community had donated over 3.2 million dollars to build a new schoolhouse and support the injured girls, as well as the students, teachers, families, and law enforcement personnel that had been touched by the tragedy.

Each of us makes choices every day that move energy into the world. What we think about expands into action in some form. Our thoughts create our reality, not only individually but also collectively. Every time we have a thought based in fear, judgment, hatred, or rage, we support the movement of those energies into the collective consciousness in which we all exist. And it doesn't matter where we direct our thoughts. When we have negative thoughts about our family members, co-workers, bosses, or leaders, we send that energy out into the world. If we think that we don't send those thoughts out against others, we should listen to our self talk: most of us will find thoughts of disappointment, anger, hatred, or rage directed at ourselves that contribute just as powerfully to the collective soup. We are all beginning to understand the many forms of eco-pollution that are threatening the life of our planet. We now know that dumping what we once thought were inert substances into toxic waste dumps has resulted in disastrous effects in the contamination of our earth and waterways. We must begin to understand that the violent thoughts we have about ourselves or about others have the same effect in the invisible world as those toxic chemicals do in the visible world. The violence we are all watching and experiencing every day in our world is the result of our collective contribution to an energetic toxic waste dump.

In the wake of the tragedy of 911, Deepak Chopra wrote a book entitled, *The Deeper Wound: Recovering the Soul from Fear and Suffering*. In this book, he cautioned us against violence in our thoughts and responses to the violence that had ripped through our country. He called for us to respond to 911 by entering deeply into our inner life and following a meditative path of "100 Days of Healing." In the introduction, he reminded us, "Great wisdom traditions tell us it is possible to go beyond suffering to reach expanded states of awareness where our personal transformation can not only bring joy to us but also heal the larger web of life." What Chopra and the wisdom teachers of all times are teaching us is that, if we want to contribute to healing the suffering of the world, we start with our own personal transformation. We start by creating "self-systems" that are whole, healthy, and happy so that we stop contributing to the invisible toxic waste dump. We re-member ourselves as body, mind, and spirit and create lives that celebrate the highest potential we hold within us as emanations of the Divine Spirit. We don't start "out there"; we start "in here."

We live in times where such remembering has never been

more vital. The spread of violence in our world is teaching us that hopelessness kills. Medical research on illnesses, like cancer and heart disease, showing that our bodies clearly respond to our thoughts and inner states is teaching us that hopelessness kills. We need an infusion of love, compassion, joy, hope, and light to balance and heal the presence of fear, rage, despair, violence, and darkness. The good news is that light is more powerful than darkness and love is more powerful than fear. It takes one candle to light a room filled with darkness and one loving thought to transform a river of fear. Our work, as we continue on our spiritual journey, is to become a force of light and love in the world—for ourselves, our children and families, our friends and co-workers, and ultimately for all of the world.

You take your place as a light worker in the world by continuing your daily practice of moving into deeper levels of self awareness and more expansive levels of consciousness. This means that you must follow the advice of Yoda and "be mindful of your thoughts." You will create thoughts based in fear, disappointment, anger, and judgment. We all do. But if you are being ever mindful of those thoughts and recognize their co-creative power in the world, you have a choice to pull the thought back and transform it with a positive affirmation and intention.

Louise Hay, author of You Can Heal Your Life, is a master of transforming negative thoughts into positive affirmations. In her work, she provides some powerful examples:

"I'm scared of being alone," becomes "I express love, and I always attract love wherever I go." "My temper is out of control," becomes "I am at peace with myself and my life." "I feel like a failure," becomes

"My life is a success." "Growing older frightens me," becomes "My age is perfect and I enjoy each new moment." Practice feeling the difference in your body when you switch from the negative thought to the positive affirmation. The negative thoughts contribute to the toxic waste dump that contaminates your life and your world; the positive affirmation changes the thought and sends out positive creative energy into the world. Simply say "eject" to negative thoughts, whether they come from within or without, and choose a new and more powerful thought to create your next experience.

Once you get better at managing your own thoughts, you can practice being a source of hope, love, and compassion for others. Refuse to engage in negative, angry, or judgmental talk with other people. When someone you meet is suffering, raise them up rather than joining them in the darkness. When your intuition tells you to reach out to someone with a message of love, do it. When Tracy was working on this book, she woke up one morning, worrying about whether it would be good enough and how our budding publishing house would support its movement into the world. Just as those feelings of doubt were trying to make a home in her consciousness, a new friend text messaged her: "God is blessing your work, and She is setting in motion the universe to receive this new creation." Tracy and her friend had not talked before he sent that message; he was probably not even consciously aware of her fears about creating this book. But the seconds he took in his day to text that beautiful message of light and love changed her instantly. It has been said that no act of kindness, no matter how small, is ever wasted. Something as simple as a thought—no matter how big or small—holds the power to change the world

We are meant to be like lighthouses in the world, holding the light of hope as a beacon in the darkness. Great leaders understand the power of hope. In one of his often quoted speeches, Robert F. Kennedy said, "Each time a person stands up for an ideal, or acts to improve the lot of others, or strikes out against injustice, he or she sends forth a tiny ripple of hope. Crossing each other from a million tiny centers of energy and daring, those ripples build a current that can sweep down the mightiest walls of oppression and resistance." Illinois senator Barack Obama has written a new book entitled, *The Audacity of Hope*. It is audacious to hope when you survey the suffering and darkness in the world today: the raging instability in the Middle East, the profound suffering in Darfur, the AIDS crisis ravaging the third world, the poverty and abuse of children in our inner cities. But through our hope and daring, each of us becomes one of those tiny centers, rippling the power and possibility of healing into the world.

At this stage of your journey, you can no longer follow the well worn way of the ordinary and visible world. You must choose thoughts of light and love and become the light that inspires others to find their way to the transformative power and promise of the invisible world. You must really give birth to your highest Self and learn to live from the very depths of your own interior. Your willingness to look through the darkness and to navigate your life by hope and not despair creates the world we will all share tomorrow. You can take small steps in your daily life to calm your fears, change your thoughts, connect with your passion and with those you love, and find ways to be in service in the world. It's not being too dramatic to say that the world is depending on you. What are you waiting for?

FULFILLMENT • HAPPINESS • CELEBRATION • PEACE

In the land beyond forever and beyond another day,
live spirits who are calling us to remember how to play.
Anne and her mommy go to visit Grandma there,
they fly there in their dreams to this land without a care.
—The Land Beyond Forever

Our mother used to say that life is God's playground; in *The Land Beyond Forever*, she and the spirits are calling us to remember how to play. As we think about making life a playground, we can't help but think about our brother Mike. Mike was the oldest child in our family and was a charismatic and life-filled spirit who always made people laugh. He loved to ski, and we shared some of our best times together skiing in Minnesota. During the rare but magical family vacations when we left the icy hills of Minnesota and headed for the powdery mountains of Colorado, Mike always made it an adventure. We will never forget the times we followed Mike dutifully to the top of the mountain for the "last run of the day." We would board one lift after another, climbing to the top of Vail Mountain. Then he would make us sit up there until the lifts had closed and all the other skiers had cleared, leaving a wide open mountain turning pink under the setting sun. When he determined that the moment was just right, he would yell something ridiculous like, "Its 'Born Free' ladies and gentleman. Last one to the bottom—!" We never heard the end of the phrase because he would take off in the lead, challenging us all to keep up. We would ski in a line, one after the other, from the top of the mountain to the bottom without stopping on his favorite run— Born Free—watching him in front of us like an elegant dancer moving effortlessly and with complete joy and exhilaration all the way down the mountain.

Mike's children remember that he also had a passion for amusement parks, and their family vacations almost always included a visit to one of the biggest and the best. Before his death, Mike bought his children lifetime passes to Disney World. After Mike became ill at the age of 31, dying at the age of 38, we were all forced to confront the fact that life is short and none of us are promised tomorrow. We recall talking with our Uncle John about Mike at the memorial. Uncle John was a former priest turned teacher, philosopher, and therapist. Nearly blind with diabetes, he lived in California, where he used to walk by the ocean on Hermosa Beach with a walking staff and his white hair and beard, looking like Moses preparing to part the Red Sea. John said that he had dreamed about Mike the night before the memorial. In the dream, Mike urgently delivered a message to him, telling him with great astonishment that "they won't even let you into heaven unless you know how to play."

Mike's life is a message for all of us about choosing how we want to live during our short time on earth. We are all "born free," happy and joyful beings that are meant to dance through life with the kind of joy and pure exhilaration we felt as we danced with Mike down that mountain. We have all experienced that feeling of joy and freedom in our lives, even if only in fleeting moments. But joy and laughter and freedom are our divine inheritance. We are born knowing how to laugh and play. Studies show that as children we laugh hundreds of times a day, but as adults we go days without laughing. In ways big and small, we allow the weight of our conditioning and the limitations of our thoughts and circumstances to imprison our spirits and kill our sense of creativity and joy. We cut ourselves off from the flow of life by the stories we create or accept about ourselves and about our lives.

In the animated movie *Happy Feet*, the young penguins are encouraged, under the coaching of an elder penguin, to reach deep inside themselves and find their "heartsong." The young penguins are told that every penguin has a song that is unique unto them and that they have to reach inside and find it from the deepest part of themselves. Children find their play naturally if we allow them the space, time, and permission to do it. Children naturally gravitate toward the things that make their hearts sing if we don't weigh them down too early with activities, schedules, goals, and responsibilities based on the futures we imagine for them. It is we adults of this world who have lost our connection to joy and play. But this "children's movie" teaches that one of the surest ways to connect with the power of joy in your life is to ask yourself what makes your heart sing. What do you do without effort and struggle that brings you joy from the deepest part of your heart? If you had all the time and money in the world, what would you do that would bring you joy and connect you with your deepest self?

In the wake of Mike's death, Tracy had to ask herself these

questions. She had graduated with honors from one of the best law schools in the country and was practicing law at the time. But she was not a happy lawyer. Parts of practicing law were interesting and challenging, and parts were rewarding. She enjoyed many of the opportunities to raise people up and empower people who were struggling. But all in all, practicing law didn't make her heart sing. What made her heart sing was her interest in understanding how we grow and learn and evolve and change. She remembered that she sailed through her psychology and theology classes in college, loving every minute of them. So as ridiculous as it seemed at the age of 37 with three small children, she left the practice of law and went back to school to get her master's degree in counseling, her heart singing through every minute of it.

Our 94-year-old Irish grandmother was incredulous. When Tracy told her with celebration that she and Meg had opened a holistic counseling center, she just kept asking, "so, you're not going to be a lawyer anymore?" Tracy's career change didn't make sense to our very practical grandmother, but, in fairness, it did not make sense to most people in the ordinary world. Giving up a safe and predictable professional career was probably not what a practical financial advisor would have suggested, and, in many ways, it has been a risk every day since. But it's never been dull. Tracy has certainly had days of self-doubt, spent worrying about tomorrow. But since she made the decision to follow her heart, each new day has miraculously taken care of itself. It has not been without some worry and struggle; the voices of "reason" inside and outside her head can get pretty loud and sound very real. But she's happy and well with four children who are learning that risk is part of life and that hopes and dreams and desires matter.

When all is said and done, we do more good for the world when we do what we love with a spirit of joy and celebration than when we do what we "should" with the weight of duty and burden. This is not to say that we all have to work in a career we love to find our joy. Some of us will make our living and find our joy through our vocation, and some will find ways to bring the joy from other areas of their lives into the work they do to make their living. The reality is that we will all have parts of our lives that are simply laborious, dull, and routine. But when we are spending more time feeling overburdened, overwhelmed, and exhausted than we spend feeling playful, optimistic, and excited, we lose the flow of joy in our life and the capacity to create and imagine new possibilities for ourselves and for the world.

The lesson then is simply to find your play, or as Joseph Campbell said, "follow your bliss." Whether it's skiing, singing, dancing, volunteering, parenting, reading to your grandchildren, hunting, gardening, cooking, decorating, organizing, reading, writing, teaching, mentoring, golfing, or playing hockey—whatever brings you joy—do it. Whatever you do that fills you with joy, laughter, optimism, and love, opens a channel of spirit that is bound to spill over into your life and into the lives of others. When Meg counsels, when Kate sings, and when Tracy teaches and writes, we are each at our best— joyful, loving channels of spirit. Being who you are truly meant to be is not work; it's play, and you are being called to remember how to play.

When you can walk through your days saying that you love your life and are deeply fulfilled by all that you do, you have discovered the secret of the universe. You have created heaven on earth for yourself, and in the process you can't help but bring that heaven into being for others. Joy is an infectious and creative force worth pursuing. Joy draws you naturally into alignment with Spirit and all your creative power and potential. You can create a happy, peaceful, and joy-filled life. What are you waiting for?

Grace

BEAUTY • ALIGNMENT • SYNCHRONICITY • MANIFESTATION

Actually, who are you not to be? You are a child of God. Your playing small does not serve the world.... We are all meant to shine, as children do. We were born to make manifest the glory of God that is within us.

— Marianne Williamson

"Let everything about you breathe the calm and peace of the soul"—during a time of particular change in her life, Tracy had these words from a Monet poster she owned painted in fourteen-inch letters across the top of her living room. The Monet poster was of his famous Water Lilies painting, and there was a beauty and stillness in that poster Tracy hoped to capture in her life at that time. On the other walls of the room, she added the words "Faith," "Laughter" "Love," "Gratitude," "Hope," "Compassion," and "Joy." Each of the words was separated by a Celtic knot design, reminding her of the interwoven and unending connection of all the parts of her life. At the time, she had three small children, worked full-time, and attended school at night. Her life was really shifting from an external focus to an internal focus, and somehow she knew that, if she was going to navigate the changes in her life and manage the speed at which things were happening, she had to connect with the energy of the Divine represented in all those beautiful words. In the energy world, words are vibration, and we can use words just like we use thoughts to come into connection with higher vibration states of being in our lives. To the outsider, painting those fourteen-inch words all around her room may have looked like a desperate cry for help—and in truth it probably was—but living under the vibration of those words in her main living area every day began to bring a feeling of calm and peace into her awareness that she could connect with in the deep stillness of her own interior.

The presence of God at work in our lives is the force connecting us to All That Is and knotting the many moving and disparate parts of ourselves and our lives into a beautiful and harmonious unity. In the deep interior of all of our beings is this river of calm and peace that we can tap into at any time because it is the very essence of who we are. The spiritual journey is a quest to connect more and more with this deep reservoir of Spirit from which we all emerged and to which we will all return. It is a reservoir of love and peace from which we can draw strength, inspiration, and restoration for our lives. At a deep level, we all know about this ever present gift. When you ask people how they were able to overcome great obstacles or endure periods of tremendous suffering or struggle in their lives, they will tell you they survived "by the grace of God." There is a force ever present in the universe that holds us up, binds us together, and provides for all of our needs as we walk through the challenges of life. We call that magnificent force Grace.

One of the dictionary definitions of grace is "an elegance of form, manner, motion or action." When we step into the mysterious power of grace, life takes on an elegant flow. There is a synchronicity about the events in our lives. We notice people and opportunities appearing each day that seem extraordinary in the visible world, but which are ordinary in the invisible world. We begin to remember with great relief that we are not in charge of the universe and that there is something bigger happening in our lives than we can even see or imagine in our humanness. We surrender our need to control and micromanage every moment of our existence. We give up needing to know what will happen tomorrow because the tomorrows we have begun to experience are filled with miracles we had not expected. When we step into the flow of grace in our lives, we awaken each morning with a feeling of openness to life, rather than a feeling of dread and protection. We trust that God is "setting in motion the universe" to receive us in love and joy, and we begin to see that it is our job to just show up with all of our unique gifts, talents, and capacities and be willing to share them with the world.

Unfortunately, we have been conditioned to separate ourselves from the flow of grace in our lives. We create limiting stories and tell ourselves that we are not worthy, not deserving, not good enough, not bright enough, not pretty enough, or not special enough in some way to receive all of the grace that God has in store for us. We think that somehow it's the other guy that God shines on and we are left to slog it out on our own, isolated and exhausted by the weight of our lives. We ask the question, "Who am I to be a recipient of God's grace?" Marianne Williamson answers us powerfully in the book *A Return to Love*:

> Actually, who are you not to be? You are a child of God.
> Your playing small does not serve the world. There is nothing

enlightened about shrinking so that other people won't feel insecure around you. We are all meant to shine, as children do. We were born to make manifest the glory of God that is within us. It's not just in some of us; it's in everyone. And as we let our own light shine, we unconsciously give other people permission to do the same. As we are liberated from our own fear, our presence automatically liberates others.

The truth that we seem unable to accept is that we don't have to earn God's grace. It is a gift that is ever present and freely given. In the Gospel of John 10:10, we read, "I have come that they may have life, and have it to the full." When you step into the power and possibilities of life supported by grace, you will find that your deepest imaginings start to show up in your life in direct measure to your capacity to believe and receive. You have to believe to receive. You have to believe that every experience in your life holds an opportunity for you to receive God's grace. You have to believe that God's angels are at work in the people you meet for you to receive the gifts God is sending you through them. You have to believe in the power of the invisible world for you to receive the miracles that God has in store for you. And as Marianne Williamson so elegantly tells us, you have to believe that you are a child of God and an emanation of Divine Spirit for you to receive the abundant blessings that are being held for you by the pure grace of God.

There is nothing more exciting than watching the exuberance of a toddler at her early birthday parties. The presents are wrapped, the candles on the cake are lit, the adults are all singing happy birthday and smiling with cameras ready, and the toddler sits amidst it all with joyful anticipation, wonder, and awe at all the fuss. She happily blows out the candles without worrying if she missed one, excitedly opens her presents without saying "you shouldn't have," and smiles for the pictures, reveling in the attention and believing in every cell of her being that she is the most important, most incredible, most remarkable human being on the planet. Toddlers are on to something. They may be the great gurus and Buddhas of all time. They know how to believe and receive.

As we leave the magic of toddlerhood, however, we all develop some kind of amnesia about our divine nature and adopt stories and patterns that deny the power of God's grace in our lives. When we sisters would get into patterns that interfered with our ability to believe and receive, our mother would look at us sternly and tell us to "get out of God's way!" When Tracy would overwork and overmanage her life like she was all alone, Mother would tell her to quit acting so ridiculously self-important and get to bed. When Meg would display false humility as a young therapist, Mom would tell her that it was not attractive to deny her God-given talent. When Kate would walk around thinking that her music didn't really matter, Mother would tell her that she was not entitled to deny the world her healing power because she was choosing to play small. Our mother knew that when we play small, buying into our small-minded stories and old insecurities, we are refusing to believe in the truth of who we are, refusing to receive God's grace, and refusing our responsibility to bring God into action in the world through us. Our very loving mother had no time for such nonsense, and we all laugh about her particular form of tough-love therapy.

Fortunately—or unfortunately—God's grace is a more patient presence in your life. God is happy to wait by the side of that river for you to remember who you are and to come back into the flow of God's grace in your life. God does not judge you or threaten you with "get it together now or else." In pure grace, God waits for you to grow tired of playing small, feeling insecure, and suffering alone in your feelings of separation. By the grace of God, we will be held and sustained through every breath of our life. When we are ready to surrender, to believe, we will receive the abundant blessings of Spirit and truly rest in the calm and peace of the soul. Enlightenment just means that we meet God at the side of that river, lay our heavy burdens down, and walk lightly through life in partnership with the Divine. God is waiting for you. What are you waiting for?

CONCLUSION

Carl Jung taught that every problem in the second half of life is a spiritual problem. He intuited what Ken Wilbur's work demonstrated—that the second half of life requires us to develop our spiritual muscles if we are going to develop fully our divine potential in the cosmic dance between Spirit and matter. The failure to feed people spiritually in our culture accounts for the epidemic of mid-life crisis, anxiety, depression, and despair. It is also creating a crisis of depression and despair among our teenagers as they look ahead and see parents living lives of quiet desperation and spiritual emptiness. We have lost any sense of vision for the second half of life beyond attaining things in the physical world, securing our retirement accounts, and dreaming about the end of work and moving to Florida. If the second half of our life is about our spiritual development, then we need a richer map for ourselves as we walk into this stage so that we can not only fulfill our own desire for lives of meaning and purpose but also become the elders and guides that our children, grandchildren, and the planet need us to be.

In our fast moving world, we want our answers to the big questions now, ready or not, and we aren't always very good at being students in life. But as Wilbur, Jung, and the ancients have taught us, our spiritual consciousness develops through steps and stages, and we need to look to those who have walked the path in front of us for guidance and direction. While the secrets of a spiritual life seem simple, walking a spiritual path has never been considered easy. In the mystery schools of ancient times and in the guru-disciple model of Eastern religious traditions, it was forbidden to give advanced spiritual teachings to a student who was not adequately prepared to handle the subtlety and the challenges of the teachings. The student's spiritual training needed to be guided and mentored through the work of a wise teacher who hand-selected students when they were ready. As the saying goes, "when the disciple is ready, the guru will appear."

So doing your spiritual work requires that you take your place as a student, allowing yourself the time to learn about your unique capacities, gifts, and resources as a co-creative agent in the Universe and to practice the skills necessary to fulfill your creative potential. As you begin your spiritual journey, give yourself permission to be a student. Take time each day for some type of reflection or contemplative practice. Cultivate your spiritual curiosity, and ask bigger questions about life and your place in it. Notice those that model an integrated spiritual life, and be willing to learn their secrets.

Unfortunately, our obsession with the young, the new, and the innovative has led us to discard our elders and too often reject the value of great teachers and the wisdom born of life's experiences. In the magic of our information age, however, the spiritual sages, masters, and guides of all times—and their writings and recordings— can be easily found in bookstores or online. You will find references to our teachers and guides throughout this book. Some of these teachers we have had the pleasure and privilege of knowing personally; others we have known through the richness of their works and writings. But they have all become sacred resources on our road to Spirit. There is a wealth of spiritual guidance available through these and other teachers, and we hope that we have shared a synthesis of the wisdom we have acquired through our studies and experiences. Whatever path you take to discovering the depths of your essence as Spirit, find teachers that enliven your search and provide you with support for your journey.

As we have stated, our culture is not designed for spiritual journeying. As you find your way, know that at times you will often feel alone and out-of-step with the world. But while we must each find our own path to Spirit, none of us came to do this work alone. We are co-creators in a cosmic web of relationships with all beings, nature, and Spirit. Spirit is calling all of us to awaken to our role in the creative process of life and to cultivate lives of awareness and attention. Help and support along the path are always available when we take the time to find them. We sisters have been blessed by support from each other as we have walked our paths side by side. Our partners have grown accustomed to our nightly conference calls, where we debrief the experiences of our days and take turns lifting each other up. At the SEND Institute, our students study and learn in a cohort model, which provides a rich and sacred community to support their work. But whether you find a family member, a program, or simply a gathering of like-minded souls, seek out people to share the journey and to support your growth.

Finally, as you enter this journey, be patient with the process. Know that just when you think you've got it you'll be invited to go deeper and begin the process again. A great master of the spiritual life, our mother, always reminded us that each step of the journey is the journey. Don't focus on the destination; just live with a profound willingness to be completely present in the Mystery you participate in every moment. We wish you peace, love, and joy on your path.

Blessings from the Three Sisters.

PROCESS AND REFLECTION

The following pages contain process questions and exercises connected to the ideas in each of the chapters of this book. You may wish to use these exercises to move more deeply into your inner life and to find your own truths. Before doing the exercises, read through the chapter that you will be focusing on, then work through the exercises relating to that chapter. You will want to have a journal, paper, colors, or markers to work through these exercises and bring the learning in and through your own body-mind system.

1. Create a ritual for starting and ending your day with an inner focus grounded in the intentions, thoughts, and beliefs you want directing your life experiences. Each day we have rituals for showering, grooming, and dressing our physical bodies for leaving the house, but how do we prepare our spiritual body to leave the house each day? Why not shower off fear, groom positive thoughts and intentions, and dress yourself for creating your day with gratitude, mystery and magic?

2. Create time to exercise and develop your inner creative muscles by making play dates for yourself three times a week for an hour of creative expression: making music, dancing, painting, writing, cooking, drawing, scrapbooking, or whatever gets your creative juices flowing. Give this time the same value or importance you would give to exercising your physical body, feeding yourself regularly, or taking your vitamins. Creativity practices are vitamins for the soul!

3. Create a list of all of the ways you are the artist choosing the conditions of your life and your environment. What colors do you love to dress in and paint on your walls? What kinds of posters and art do you choose? What kind of jewelry do you wear? What type of furniture do you like? Who do you spend your time with? What kinds of music do you listen to? The number of choices you make as a creative artist in your life is staggering—from the moment you open your eyes in the morning you are choosing thoughts, colors, roads, friends, songs, schedules, foods, and on and on. Start to notice your choices and make them with clarity and intention to reflect your deepest dreams and your greatest possibilities.

1. Imagine the freedom to be yourself at all times and the inner strength you would have if you gave yourself permission to be your true self. Begin getting to know yourself by answering the following questions:

    a. Are you more introverted or extroverted?

    b. Do you prefer to gather information about the world using your five physical senses or do you prefer to use your intuition?

    c. Do you like to make decisions using facts and logic or gut feelings and emotions?

    d. Do you like to make plans spontaneously in the spur of the moment, or do you like to have time to make plans and decisions long in advance?

2. Imagine that the world needs exactly the positive gifts and qualities that are connected to your truest self. How would it feel to tell the truth about your positive gifts and qualities knowing that your expression of those gifts will make the world more complete? List ten positive qualities you know about yourself beginning each sentence with the words "I AM . . ." For example: I am funny; I am sensitive; I am smart; I am strong; I am determined; I am loyal.

3. Imagine that your favorite characters in history or in your favorite movie, play, book, or story are parts of you. Name three of your favorite characters and journal about the qualities they show you about yourself.

4. Imagine every person in your life has been carefully selected to allow you to learn about who you are. Sometimes we learn through experiences that we perceive as positive and sometimes through experiences we perceive as negative. Name three people that helped you know who you are through a positive experience and three people that helped you to know who you are through a negative experience. Journal about the lessons you learned from all of them.

1. Can you trust that the world is a friendly place—God's playground on earth—and that God will support you in bringing forward your heart's desires? Spend some time writing down three wishes or dreams that come from your heart and think about how you might begin to make room in your life for those wishes and dreams to come true.

2. If the ability to trust life is your birthright, imagine what it would feel like to end your relationship with self-doubt and fear and to start a new relationship with self-love and trust? On a new piece of paper make a list of three fears or self-doubting beliefs. Place that list next to the list of three wishes and dreams you wrote down in exercise one. Hold each list in your hands and feel the change in your body, your breathing, and your mood when you look at each list. Which sheet of paper makes you feel tense and constricted? Which sheet makes you feel excited, creative, open, or alive? Trust the wisdom of your body to lead you toward what is truly you. Now rip up the list of fears and self-doubts and write down ten things that would change if you really let those fears go and followed your dreams.

3. Trust that struggle is a sign that you are outgrowing an old or limiting belief and frustration is a sign you are getting ready to do something new. If that is true, then write down something that is a current struggle or frustration for you and journal about what in that situation you are outgrowing or ready to change. Now write about the new ideas or experiences you would like to make room for in your life.

1. Practice watching the trees to learn the secret of letting go. Draw a tree and place five to ten leaves on it. Place a thought, belief, or behavior that is no longer serving you on each of the leaves and meditate on letting go of them as gently as the trees let go of their old leaves in the fall. Now, under and around the base of the tree, write five to ten new replacement thoughts, beliefs, or behaviors that your true self is eager to create in the next few months. Let these new ways of thinking and behaving be the soil that will grow the next season of leaves on your tree. Let go of the old to make room for the seeds of the new!

2. Name three or more ways Mother Nature encourages us to
    let go by her example, while reassuring us of the new life to
    come. Hint: How does Mother Nature show us to let go and
    trust in the cycles of the sunset and sunrise, trees and seasons,
    caterpillars and butterflies? Meditate on the miracles present
    in these transitions and notice yourself more willing to flow
    gently with the changes in your own life.

3. In your physical environment practice the art of letting go by
    identifying three areas of your home and choosing ten things
    in each room to throw away or give away. Let go of the old
    and make room for new abundance to come into your life.
    Home organizers and Feng Shui masters teach that if your
    drawers and closets are jammed with stuff there is no way to
    make room for new clothes, new ideas, new energy, or new
    channels of money to enter your life.

1. Identify something in your life that you are doing that is a new behavior or challenge for you. Would it be easier to believe in your ability to succeed at this new thing if you accepted the toddler theory, knowing you will learn with practice? And if you allowed yourself to make mistakes, take breaks, and ask for help? Write yourself a letter encouraging your new learning and offering loving support and acceptance.

2. Find an inspirational saying or affirmation with the word "BELIEVE" in it. Write it, paint it, download it, or buy it—and put it up in your bedroom or bathroom where you will see it each morning and evening, allowing it to really soak into your consciousness. Read it many times a day and feed that new thought to your heart and mind.

3. Make a list of all the beliefs about life that you learned from family, friends, school, church, and culture. Examine that list and see which of those beliefs you want to continue to BELIEVE are true for you. For each old belief you want to throw away, write a new, positive statement on what you now BELIEVE.

1. List one thing that your heart really longs for in your life and your head tells you is too risky or not possible. It might be creating a more loving relationship with a family member, going back to school, or finding a new place to live or work. After you identify the thing you are longing for, write a letter from your heart to your head explaining your dream and just how important it is to you. Let your head know how your heart would feel with this change coming into your life and all the miracles that would happen if it became true. After writing the letter, meditate for a few minutes on that longing as if it were already done, allowing your heart to wrap up that longing with love.

2. List three relationships in your life where you wish to find the gift of forgiveness. Write a letter to each of those people either asking them for forgiveness or offering your forgiveness. In the letter, express your deepest wishes for the healing of the relationship and the love you would like to bring into your heart. You don't need to send the letter; just open your heart to the possibility of forgiveness.

3. Take out a blank piece of paper and draw a large circle as big as the page. Using colors or markers, write your name in the center of the circle. Now inside the circle, write all the conditions that feed your heart and make you feel warm, safe, vibrant, and alive. How many hours of sleep do you need? What foods nourish your body? What people bring you alive? What colors, music, work, activities make you happy? Fill the inside of the circle with all the conditions that make your heart sing. Now hang this paper where you will see it knowing that these are the conditions that will make you grow and thrive. You may want to share them with the people in your life you love. But remember, you are your own gardener and need to create these conditions for yourself. You must be sure you tend to your heart with love each day by giving it the things it needs.

1. Name three people in history or living today that symbolize hope for you. Spend some time thinking about the life challenges they faced and the qualities they possessed that allowed them to come forward as a hope-filled person. Use these people as lighthouses to light the way and encourage you during moments of doubt and despair. If you are facing a difficult time in your life right now, you may want to place a picture of the person in a place you will see it to remind you to press on.

2. Write a note to someone you care about who is struggling with despair in an area of their life. Let them know that you are aware of their struggle and raise them up with your words of hope and encouragement.

3. We have learned that hopelessness injures our spirit, takes our energy, and negatively affects our physical bodies. Identify areas of your life where you hold a repetitively negative thought, and turn the thought around to create a positive affirmation. For example, "There is never enough time," becomes "I have enough time each day for the things that are important to me." Each time the negative thought comes into your mind or speech, use that affirmation to turn it around, and watch how the new thought opens up new possibilities in your life.

1. Make a collage filled with pictures, activities, and words that represent the things that make you feel joyful. Do you give yourself permission to spend your time pursuing joy in your life? If you are not playing or laughing enough, you now have a picture of all the things that move you toward joy and can start bringing some of those activities or experiences into your life each day.

2. Identify a comedy or a comedian that makes you laugh, rent the movie or see the show, and give yourself permission to take a break in your day to enjoy the pure pleasure of laughter.

3. Think about the things you do for play that really bring you joy. Now quickly write down all the stories in your head that stop you from doing these things in your life on a regular basis. Whose voices are in your head telling you that play is silly, frivolous, or just for kids? How have you gotten stuck in never-ending routines of productivity and seriousness? Whose permission do you need to play? Decide today that you are the only one in charge of your "joy-meter" and make sure that it registers an experience of joy each day.

1. Spend a few minutes meditating about the power of grace in your life. Now write the word grace at the top of a piece of paper and answer the following questions:

   a. What is the color that represents grace for you?

   b. What is a song that reminds you of grace?

   c. What image do you see when you think about grace?

   d. What do you feel in your body when you meditate on grace?

   Write the answers to these questions on your paper and you have now created a "grace file" in you mind that will help you to connect more consciously with the power of grace in your life.

2. Name three experiences where you felt the presence of grace in your life. Write a letter as if you are telling a friend about the miracles of those experiences, sharing with great excitement about all of the details and surprising turns of events that came forward to support you in unexpected ways. Let yourself really feel the power of those experiences and know in the depth of your heart how the power of grace is at work in your life when you allow yourself to trust and "get out of God's way!"

3. Settle into a quiet place, light a candle, and put on some music that brings you a feeling of calm and peace. Now close your eyes, breathe deeply and evenly, and imagine that you are walking in a beautiful, green, light-filled meadow where you meet with a wise and loving presence—an angel, a deceased loved one, Jesus, God, or whatever figure represents love, compassion and grace for you. Imagine sitting along the side of a beautiful river with that figure. The figure gently and lovingly invites you to release anything you are worrying about into the river—allowing the worry or burden to flow gently to God. With each burden you release to God you feel lighter and easier, trusting that God's grace will bring forward all of the circumstances you need to address that situation. Spend as much time as you need resting in the grace of this presence, and return to this meditation whenever you feel heavy or troubled.

MUSIC FOR INSPIRATION

We have included a selection of music from our CD *Transcendence* in the back of this book to support your practice and learning. At the SEND Institute we promote integrated, whole body learning, knowing that we all learn differently—some through reading, some through processes, and some through music, movement, and vibration. Give yourself the opportunity to read the book, practice with the process exercises, and listen to the music to inspire your journey.

ABOUT THREE SISTERS

THREE SISTERS PUBLISHING HOUSE

Three Sisters Publishing House is the creative force of Flynn sisters Tracy, Kate, and Meg. Three Sisters is committed to publishing projects promoting integrated, holistic growth and learning—encouraging people to live with compassion, creativity, consciousness, and connection. The Flynn sisters also operate the SEND Institute and New Directions Counseling & Training. Together they author a regular spiritual-emotional health column in *Among Women Magazine*. The sisters work, teach, and live in Minnesota.

Tracy is trained as a lawyer and counselor and holds a law degree from the University of Minnesota, a master's degree in counseling psychology from the University of St. Thomas, and a bachelor of arts degree in psychology and theology from the College of St. Benedict.

Kate is an elementary school educator and licensed administrator with a master's degree from Saint Mary's University of Minnesota and a bachelor of arts degree in education from the College of St. Benedict.

Meg is a licensed marriage and family therapist with a master's degree in counseling psychology from the University of St. Thomas

135

and a bachelor of arts degree in psychology and theology from the College of St. Benedict.

For book orders or information, visit our website at www.threesisterspublishing.com.

SEND™ INSTITUTE

For readers seeking opportunities for integrative learning based on the principles and teachings of this work, Three Sisters invites you to join us for programs and workshops designed to support personal transformation and spiritual growth through the SEND™ Institute (Spiritual, Emotional, iNtuitive Development). The cornerstone of the SEND Institute is the SEND Program, a six-module, cohort-based learning opportunity that empowers students to become creative agents in their lives and in the world. The SEND Program assists students in identifying their unique gifts and capacities, provides tools for emotional healing and spiritual growth, and sends students out inspired to live their passion and share their light in the world.

For more information on workshops and programs visit our website at www.sendinstitute.com.